Clio's Ground

Clio's Ground
New & Selected Poems

Fergal Gaynor

Shearsman Books

First published in the United Kingdom in 2025 by
Shearsman Books Ltd
PO Box 4239
Swindon
SN3 9FN

Shearsman Books Ltd Registered Office
30–31 St. James Place, Mangotsfield, Bristol BS16 9JB
(this address not for correspondence)

EU AUTHORISED REPRESENTATIVE:
Lightning Source France
1 Av. Johannes Gutenberg, 78310 Maurepas, France
Email: compliance@lightningsource.fr

www.shearsman.com

ISBN 978-1-84861-959-3

Copyright © Fergal Gaynor, 2025.

The right of Fergal Gaynor to be identified as the author of this work
has been asserted by him in accordance with the
Copyrights, Designs and Patents Act of 1988.
All rights reserved.

CONTENTS

3 Paeans / 9
For Ed / 12
The Octagon / 13
Runes / 24
Cork's Lough / 34
Twinning / 37
The Tower / 39
Las Meninas / 42
After J.S. Bach's 'Musical Offering' / 43
Cubist Portrait of Hippolytus / 49
2 Futurologies / 59
The Furthest Reaches / 61
Guyenne Sketch / 62
On Either Side
of a Blank / 67
Sudoku / 68
Excerpt from 'A New History of Printing' / 69

Notes / 74
Acknowledgements / 75

'I feel less tyrannised by the present day.'

—Iggy Pop on his love of Gibbon's *Decline and Fall*

for Marja,

who, among other things, gave me Finland

3 Paeans
(for the Savonian Woods)

1.

Iron-blue
columns,

orange-glow,
from the forge –
pine shafts,

green needle
plumes.

Here is a rock.
Uninterested
in further form.

The sun strikes
Saimaa's
flowing sheen:

sparkles,
millions.

2.

Who would extol
the pillars
of Aachen,
among

these free
uprights?

Who
in berried aisles,
would dwell on vaults
of porphyry and gold?

Who regret
the smoke of incense,
on this sun-patched pavement,
of vetch,
chanterelle,
repeated lift
of citron
wings?

3.

In the brief high summer

the son mounts
the green lawn,
to the villa.
He is brown
as Väinämöinen.

Between the striped
birches
the sun paints
the lake,
itself,
tangerine –

a disc above,
below, a lozenge.

Cloud-reflecting
white meandering lines
enclose the cobalt-blue water,
the darker island
tumuli.

Sky of evening
sets copper sparks
among the basalt-clasping pines,
kindles
the waves.

There is no steamboat
flaring birch logs
in its iron bowel,
there are no ribbons
on the pine trunks.
In the brief high summer
piano notes from the window,
music among the trees.

For Ed
(who asked about 'difficult poetry')

Do not commit
these things
to print.

It is not that they would
betray you,

but that they would
betray themselves.

Commit them
in their brightness
to memory.

Send out instead
ciphers,

though nothing
may become
of ciphers.

The Octagon

When the wind is southerly, I know
a hawk from a hand saw.

I

On the hillside
the house is empty –
where is the shepherd?
In the fold
the flock shifts –
where is the one
who brings calm to the sheep?
In the wilderness
in the place of wild beasts
he searches the ravines.
Gripping his staff
he stares in the fissures –
night is not far off.
In the hillside house
the fire is unlit,
the sheep unwatched –
where is the shepherd?

II

Our bastards anointed

on such bodies possessed
never laid hands

thought's bright foot
stubbed on the horizon

from shaping tongue
inarguable forms

the womb mistaken
for a multitude of infants

made of light

Matchless Lucifers

by divine numbers' stream
strike quick silver

plumb jobs in the underworld
the angels underpaid

reach of bronze Mars
into compound and wedding crystal

further change of state
to license the Lawgiver

for a limited future

Frantic bondsmen

bind quick nets
for careering bees

Beelzebub dust
in the songster's gullet

dung-rollers pile
unsoil the olive

ungovernable rise
ephemera to be fed on

like children

Jet you higher airs!

Stream over tonguing winds!
Re-stitch the cloven peoples!

Purge low circulations!
Draw up all purer drops!

Un-herald the striking flash!
Stir opiate clouds!

Cut stars from their ether!
Douse earth with fiery seeds

without germ

Start

intimate
shoots

reconstitute
the borders

bloom
uncontained

mature
the fantastic

nursery

Doctor

patient
accounts

disprove
pastorals

plot
loyalty

incorporate
the fabulous

decline

For the fat decade

has splayed the lord
that cries and culls

for the bank-holing martins
have tracked the ore

for the unknown voice
has benighted the pawns

for the stranded eel
has slipped through the grass

into sand

And clubbing jacks

have heaped black drift
against the heart's door

and hide has been sought
by the ruler of game

and the enveloped outed
to lights of exposure

and the cosmos reflected
in a bubble's iridescence

swelling swelling

III

Light dims,
Aldebaran, alone,
starts up the slope.
Night will fall with violence.
Now eyes widen
seeing less –
and the ear opens,
listening
for a footstep,
for a hand on the latch.

Runes

I.

health
a holy well
a wet hollow

many
pending
at screens

the dead knowledge
or else
a science of death

wet leaves
pressed
glenfuls

how not to be
where you are

II.

scattered
colonies
of words

this is dry work
with little camaraderie
and Rome fallen

by the rushes
we were married
with a river for priest

word may yet come
I have gambled on its being
'amor'

spring comes
scribbling greenery

III.

Chartres –
chrysalis
glorious glassy

neutral space
house
fit for devils

bricks plaster
industrial paint –
the will to charity

public house
scriptorium
court of black mouths

like the sun the spirit
erring through the signs

IV

in the world
carved away
the poem

remains
of Beuys' effort
of the artist

the ceremony ended
the doors are closed
the doors are closed

sunshine
ever fleeting
and enough

I miss Meliboeus
I miss his quiet flute at evening

V

polaroids
of a life
worse forgotten

anything –
a prison-house
turned inside-out

the headland –
how is it
still there?

once servants
you betrayed them
you serve me

Berlin
will not be filled

VI

Sheltered
from the sea
the harbour

withdrawn
from the harbour
the land

hidden
in the land
this

sun holding hollow.

Absent
in our exposure
to the sea

absent
in our anticipation
in the harbour

absent
in our meetings
on the land

brief
in this
sun holding hollow.

VII

Black access
shafts caves tunnels
spire's descent

estate walkways
white portico
a line of faces

autumn
unseals
branching chambers

rabbinical digit
tracks
'The Origins of Management'

in front of
electronic portal

VIII

'even the homeless
have time'
states Debord

such time
as is stored
in Paris Ville

the countryside
being timeless
the Cité

a timebomb
an hour-on-hour press
of anticipation

so to trading
stocks and futures

IX

Black moth
white butterfly
as missives

on the horizon
spinning
the furious top

what is not
is what is
yet to be

so a child comes
a boat approaches
presently

could time be remade
by waiting?

X

poetry
as production
line

for an age now
art
outsourced

tiny fingers
sharp reflexes
good for such work

space
grows
in the library

as if a fire burnt
as if green things

Cork's Lough

*The kind of motion and place of the body
are determined according to the nature
of the body.*

Tangentially the sustained crash of metal passage
traffic of encased bodies liberating thissamebody
from anywhere into anywhere a line covers
nothing this line's not-ends extend not-yet-forever
science too slow we must learn from the artists
and accelerate that is exchange anything this strip
of violence but entropy but inertia but if you can
spare a time
here it curves away
into closure (as when a line
returns to itself, that is, a body) –

here is a reserve.

Salutary round,
on the water's green girdle
easy concourse
of geese and pedestrian,
freewheeling cyclist,
recyclist, epicyclist,
past meditative anglers,
eyeing the other
element's
occluding body,
a turn of bodies
reveal at their own pace
the around-each-curve,
as the breeze enters

with hermetic birds
and the leaves utter
that once
in holiday weather
Pearse rising Corkonian Corkery:
'you'd think they'd drain it.'

Overlooking,
the 1950s
windows
are blinded,
but only kind sunshine enters
this unused hollow
to light the swans' self-ceremonies,
the parabolising tennis ball
lifted from a hurley,
metabolism
of shouts across distance,
of brightness off water,
of green lounging,
of the birds' ascents
and descents,
of the hidden source,
of the island's dark thicket,
setting
freedom;
so tell the roamers
that they are welcome,
but there is one law:
that every carp or rudd
they pierce
and lift towards
a gasping death
must be returned to life.

Night's return
starts the mirrored illuminations,
and beams lance
on the reconstituted waters,
seize momentarily
the duck's form,
the near trunk,
something on the water,
in one sweep.
But the floating swan
remains,
a pale cypher,
and the dark island
recedes, gathers
in upon itself,
a hunched obscurity.
Only stewards cross
to the moist entangled
nesting ground,
treading soft-footed around
the eggs' mottled
microcosms.
In the dead season
they place at its edge
the image of a child,
in view of the city's
transposition
exposed,
open-armed
in the cold
to the firmament's
slow silent
revolution.

Twinning
(for the Celtic Tiger)

Cread i an ruaig soar thoraibh
Buala buan a mbona?
(What is this human tumult
with so much fell destruction?)

Shandon Tower
that grand old dame
stript of her decorous urns
shall earth never sleep?
the jackhammers strike no
though Murphy nods
and Mahony and Mahood
seeds in the shifting ground
knowing nor 'bove nor below
so that growth grows
cancerously internal
ah my dead republic!

Oh city galvanic!
foundations sunk
in crab ooze in bog
its fibrous limits
filigree the green
roads shining scars
skirt sleeperless tumuli
the city lifts!
as steel tendrils tauten
we enter breathless air
two hundred thousand souls
rise from their birth beds!

Breeze over the grey Lee
history its shadow
time was streets recalled
Blarney's wry flâneur
traffic ate the time
the groves of sleep are felled.

Engineless mills
where priestwool was wound
a harvest of hands
broke rosary and rota
the hour comes with no bell
we turn on ourselves.

The Tower
(for the Elysian Building)

We could, I suppose,
                knock it –
                              then rebuild,
downward,

past where
    bandoned desirables wait the promised
    return;

past where
    daily alarums rolled motorised columns,
    centreward, restarting commerce, keeping
    dull occupation;

past where
    flat roofs made plastic the sunny ideal, wide
    asphalt let cruise the new-minted steel;

past where
    bronze, uniformed head, proportioned to the
    public park, oversaw black action, the lost,
    green what-might-have-been;

past where
    citizenry again made exhibition of self, rising
    to familiars in imperial glass;

past where
    Boole's buildings sizing, from 45 to 49, the
    rational road took toll quotient, gate arrivals
    counted all their bones;

past where
> meaty dividends raised rich piles, off-isle,
> high, dry, aweigh from wick'd smell,
> guttural hands, low tidal draughts;

past where
> Mangan's four-faced metre failed, at
> steeple's foot, to levy, with unsolemn clang,
> the levelled Mahony;

past where
> the little courses culverted, and the great,
> estate was extended, ishka fay holluv laid
> over, by mall, parade and street;

past where
> Coppinger cross of the gentrified chief,
> close courser of planters, marauded by
> mortgage;

past where
> the virgin's privateers, energetic undertakers,
> divided gentle land and upstart bodies, setting
> star form over wandering flood;

past where
> London tower stories decked handsomely in
> silks a landloping ape;

past where
> portable Rome for port opportune, for
> aedification, had set stone boot;

past where
> the netted hostman, Barry's bondsman,
> tracked seafarers, speckled and flash;

past where
> monastery managed, so Munster developed;

past where
> river's solvent lees stored small charge, counts
> half-gotten, horns of ould potency;

past where
> stone forecasts raised the sun, gone under
> world's end of the western road;

to probe
> through all-forgiving depths, the
guileless earth, to stone,

wine-dark, steel grey, green as the wrack-wreathed waters,

waiting, to be lifted, high into human air,

singular, demonstrative,

and not

before

time.

Las Meninas

A world peopled with images,
what else would a painter paint?

> *

Being's joinery,
it appears,

serves not
to compartment –

the screens, doors,
mirrors, frames,

space by space,
extending.

> *

How else might a dwarf wait
near a princess,
but by partitions?

Or a retainer
cross a foot
to a dog's back?

Or decorated Velázquez
deliberate on
royal shadows,

fixed in their place,
looking
as we look?

After J.S. Bach's *Musical Offering*

1. Canon a 2

In der Kammer in Potsdam

behind the clear
           clock
                      face
that measures directs
courtier positions
and the State
the universe works

HERR

Rex Princeps Supremus
Majesté
Allergnädigster König

here is a problem

the fall
       through
              coloured tones
resisting solution
halt to the old art
of canon
scandal
among the orders

herr
67 jahre
ein mann

traveller alone
in Thuringian woods
still dark enough to hold
a woodcut devil
or worse

the voice of God
from the organ-loft
bustle
        and dissonance
dutiful overlay
of unpleasing codes
compendious

thoroughgoing business
of brown things
tables, masts, beer, pens,
churches, ropes, dark bread,
chartered water

productive of girth
bürgerlich
hunched in prayer
frowns
for the grace of his children
there are ten laws

what comes not by industry
is insubstantial
its light
though the light of liberty
the light of fools

king sun

the joined vault
may be fallen into
divine reason
lost among the stars
their singing
without cadence

I have raided the closet
I have gained knowledge of these things
Reinken Kepler Paracelsus

The King Laughs

and there are straight streets
wheat in the barns
unforced harmony
from Netherland to steppe
a plane stamped
by wheeling geometries
army after army

he must insist
upon his estate

a frame
thrown on grass
star-shaped
make it strong
and inside
enclearment
the obscure thicket
felled
while the law
         leafs
              proliferous

HERR

I have augmented
this problem
not just as notes are lengthened
(here is a multiplication of notes)
but as a king may
augment his Realme
in Rycesse, Welth, and Prosperyte
here is a wealth of difficulty

familial puzzles
the canonical ten
a fête galante
at time of departure
the old volutions
mirrors and number
returns
of Rome's failure

so the sun descends
being on a wheel
and in winter-light
fortune is tarnished
the instruments
laid out
subject of the king
become a plea

Eli Eli
canon perpetuus
ich kann nicht anders
as an offering made

2. Trio Sonata

Prussian history
not yet
absolute
there is space in the bureau
for a fluteful of breath
and its spilling over.

The doors are closed
to day's business
French windows
open
to the breeze
and to gardens
holding light
after the sun's going
from the heavens.

Now
the light of candles
courteous
kind to artifice
so that on painted blue
the sprays of leaves
and lucent shadows
may move
in the tonic stream
unfolding and withheld
resonant in memory
in the not-yet
remembered.

It is by grace
and must be welcomed
as is natural
and a law.

Tokaji is poured
in Brandenburg crystal
with genteel words
sweet things for the ear
and before the candle ends
the clock gives measure
time like a heartbeat
and near the windows
a leaf-crowned youth
soft lustrous
on a spindle-legged chair
the sun is sitting.

Cubist Portrait of Hippolytus

Hippolytus a jolly huntsman was,
That wont in charet chace the foaming Bore…
His father fierce…
Who ail in rage his Sea-god syre besought,
Some cursed vengeance on his son to cast…
Both charet swift and huntsman ouercast,
His goodly corps on ragged cliffs yrent,
Was quite dismembered…
Them brought to Æsculape, that by his art
Did heal them all againe, and ioyned every part.
  —Spenser, The Faerie Queene

In the instant, after,

after the bang, that begins, the crash,

to the roar of the long waves, sea animal, Hippolytus cast, horse-powered to helpless,

and his careering car, on hard matter, scattered, bones, flesh, more fluid stuff, metal

mixed, without prejudice,

on the rocks.

In that instant, instant of ink-dark

upsurge, to the earth's pound, of breakers, shell strewing, loud,

of beasts' bolt, machine veers, unharnessed from mastery, wheels free,

and the charioteer, this integral man, credit-worthy,

sound stock of faithless Theseus, the popular, of breastless Hippolyta's line, consigned, haphazard, to particles,

sprayed, as stars are, on a plane.

In that instant, starts

the Goddess, the chaste one, at the cry, reaching her ear, speedier than sight,

of the stricken, picked in flight, her devotee, strict darling, dismantled of manhood,

and already on the shore, her foot's shining contour, slipped through the windstream,

touching down, and quick in her train, soft bathers, exchanging bank for beach, to stare,

too late! aftermath's account,

all too plain, on the table, laid out.

Instantly, in advance,

in advance of a scream, from virgin viewers, solicited by horror, the Huntress,

Artemis, the clean-limbed, by eye imperious, stilling the Oceanids,

as with a cry, bay-echoing, Iris, the swift one, bridger of distance,

is summoned, skates, on technicolour film, to arrive at the ear,

of Hygiene's sire, the Healer, so flash back, quicker than ideas, the pair,

to the theatre, of blood and stone,

frozen chorus, and the one brought low.

When said Leto's offspring, who delights, as delights the Delian, in the strike of darts:

'When that engine of miracles, prodigious plant, store of restoration,

conveyed, from its mine of know-how, by a snake, is yours, Son of consumed Coronis,

why not? When promise radiant, guarantee of joyous growth, swelling notability,

is smashed, by no necessity, but bossed, by economy of chance, why not?

When this happy sportsman, excelling in chase, fearing nor boar nor wildcat,

dutiful in divine returns, is marked by a lascivious tongue, low competition,

of faithless father, and the sea's ranks, for sudden wreck, Son of Phlegyas,

whose skin is lit by flame, encircled, underground, why not?

When his value, to me is such, and no word recorded, that prohibits, save, what I say now:

let limit be crossed, let flesh,

beloved life, rebind, wheels rewhirl,

why not?'

At which, in instant assent, the silent Helper, extends ability, over parts all strewn,

strives to assemble, what had been, hunts the elements of recreation, gathers

germs of a new nature, picks through the debris, uncovers precious pieces, pieces

intact, so precious, of the inert prince, laid under curse, undesert, that is:

1. crown, segment of, as raised, by rights, with official marks, of majesty, seat of merit, pedestaled, holding position, as property, parent-arranged, patented, owed deference, source of propriety, proper, etc;

2. foot, nearly whole, left, as held the level, one among the huntsmen, without precedence among trees, obeisant to the logic of the chase, teamster, subordinate to the outcome, effectual, etc;

3. hand, damaged, right, the generous, not incognizant of misfortune, uncareless with the poor, giving, on feastdays, from wealth, the welcome coin, groat met with gratitude, extended through agents, spread kingdom-wide, manipulative, etc.

4. limbs, various, torso, as if tooled, well-exercised, fitted to tasks, powering, quick fixers of fault, trim, sufficiently strong, without excess, exact, etc;

5. heart, part of, propelling the greater, ever ready, ever active in whatever act, beating faster for early rising, never pausing, beating late and hard, whenever required, exemplary organ, busy, etc;

6. eyeball, whole, undeceived, undistracted in the tangle, reductive of the scene, to need and the matter, narrowed, focused on the quarry, seeing its end only, directing the weapons, sharp, etc;

7. hand, left, section of, as cut, the dispatcher, dealing the blow, to the wounded, without hope, never shirking, kindness at the kill, humane, definite, etc;

8. ear, entire, receptive to noise, background hiss, aware of wavesound, the abyssal sea, (the upsurger, the wall-assaulter, the nightcrier, the eater of piles, the robber of deposits, the sacker of shore), register of threat, prescient, resonant shell, doomful, etc;

9. in addition, sinew, muscly cable, nervous thread, small bones, numerous – what remains, too fluid, smashed, milled, mangled, or unrecognized in the physick art, he passes over, and

modelling, with prebiotic slop,

makes order, and the mould of man.

For an instant, long instant, hushed, but for surf sound, the bright nymphs, like starlets,

surrounding, fixed by the scene, anticipant of escape, the hero's, from certainty of Hades,

Asclepius, unpicker of mysteries, worker of wellness, applies it, that therapeutic twig,

sappy rod, reviver and sustainer, same pass, through deceptive port, of fleeing Aeneas,

until, sensational to behold, begins, hinging and adhesion, pieces

linking to pieces, joints generate, circuits, networks knit, reparations spread,

throughout the frame, and all, immortal, witnessing the apparition, wonder:

will spirit return, instincts spark, fell

instant reverse, and the course of death?

Instantly, twitchings, tremblings in one sector, upturn, of a finger,

heart runs and syncopations, thrilling the speculators, but not him presiding,

true son of Apollo, prescribing, in all things, the measured, right ratio,

preferring despair, cold certainty of sense, to flaring hope, images on the horizon,

realist, with a cold eye, he turns from the experiment, its determinate state,

and, addressing the Mistress, explains, how marvellously indeed, each

part, executive, active organ, has now revived, and fleshly chamber,

twin-valved, contains the multiplicity, yet essence effective, unity to do, is lacked, the inner drive, of living bits,

the whip, and will that steers.

Long wait, for mortal woe, for sighs, sent up, from tenants of the earth,

a lockout, sensed above, but listenership, directly, for divine wish, celestial aid,

as evidenced by instant arrival, to the shapely slayer of Adonis, much mourned,

of Maia's smiling son, well-heeled Hermes, the Exchanger, enterprise's agent,

the breeze of whose passing, across the highwayed world, is, at every crossroads,

felt, simultaneously, and sooner than desire, for resolution, inflates the breast,

of Aristo, tourer of green ranges, his head is there, inclined, receiving the message,

lips curved, the limit crosser, ringer of the world's blue dial, and, exchange once ceased,

the god, as a leaf, fallen, on pavements of Dodona, sacred to Dione, breeze-caught,

engages the air, lifts, weightless,

whirling upwards, disappears.

To reappear, immediately, the Mediator, to drop, in planet-hopping pumps,

through cruder air, from ether, earthwards, warm Gaea's reserve, where, near Arcadian Alpheus, his spilling, from cool obscurity, to Helios' flaming gaze, in which all things are fine, and clear,

into the Ionian well, wise Hodios, the roadster, alights, a stalk to pluck, of fennel,

that tastes the salt breeze, and straight, the ground's hold, releasing, takes the short leap

to Helos, in Elis, its mists and marshes,

where Heleia, the lovely, is loved, and feared.

Transfer, at dream speed, to different scene, boots brushing alder leaves, the god's drift,

over shifting field, of fog, miasma, hunched tree forms, half-hidden, their roots ooze-knitting,

nest of amphibia, mewling fowl, eels that slip unseen, until, cruising, over land's heart,

tree-dark, Helos' hidden core, he, the hoverer, descends, into twilit depression,

a breeze, about the Psychopomp whirling, clearing below, uncultivated growth,

rude, up-thrusting complex, other barriers

to light, and the detective eye.

Again, instant change, as the god, going under, under thicket dome, entering

inner space, huge hollow, cavernous, where shifting glows, mercurial,

among branch-shadows, like diagrams of nerves, thrown on a screen, flickering across tree-walls, now dark, condensed, enclosing, now swelling, fluorescent, magnified,

chutes, with grace, effortless descent, and halts, to wait, over water,

a mirroring pool, dark as past time, on whose surface a mix, of silver gleam and mist,

like fog searched by lamps, lingers, where twin-horned Semele, of the wandering beams,

Helios' other half, after Night's interval, long journey over lands, alone,

long gazing to catch, only glimmers, of her visage, change reflected, off small waters,

glamour of silver leaves, visits religiously, bending, like Narcissus,

beloved of double-voiced Echo, over moving image, to fix, in eyes' aperture

the features focused, returning look,

the semblance that assumes a self.

Return, to the first scene, return,

to the set, of stone and sea, the tide now

in free flood, the progress, in waves, from crest to crash, repeating,

the first instant, the singular, catastrophe,

return, to the spectacle on the rocks, the shocked looks, about the fallen,

of those, rooted by remains, locked, on the image of disaster, fast holding, to the parts,

rearranged, in a form that conforms, human-like, trim, but unliving, so, the immortals, suspended, unknowing, that elsewhere, unshaken, shorthaired Hermes, Apollo's cajoler,

has, in his fennel flask, caught the impossible, rendered the remedy, brought aid

to the dismayed band, and he is there, toe first, tipping the earth, arm-length from Artemis,

displaying, like a flower bouquet, the prize pursued, in its plain case, plucked

by the Alpheus, Olympian stream, the moonshine, marvellous, unprohibited,

by Phoebe's decree, and precipitously, it is in the Healer's hands, dabbing on orbs

that stare at nowhere, pressing to lips,

parched, by no lack of water.

Oh golden moment, it stands, in standard, if invalid, shape, a jerking assemblage,

Hippolytus revenant, recognizable, if transformed, a polymorph, immortal diamond,

faceted, the parts remastered, centrally powered, about his head steers, with assessing eyes,

marking the personages, their rank and worthiness, pausing at the goddess,

glacially he bows, and, unarcing, from earth away, he launches his sight,

out into blue heights, towards the upper orbits, of spheres unchanging, province

of the gods, reaching, a fat-free arm, splayed hand, along the trajectory, of vision, each finger parted, as if, this union, of fleshly particulars, the clashing atoms

of the cosmos, might incorporate, harness stars, at which, from their nebulous thrones,

start, as at violence, Titanic,

the celestials, shocked, anticipating

2 Futurologies

I

Spring was scheduled,
but nothing happened –
something had been
removed from the earth.
We hadn't realised…
pleading innocence
to empty skies.

Some prospered,
or felt they had –
their children came not
to their deathbeds.
Difficult
in any case:
the machinery
to keep them dying
filled the room –
wondrous, transparent,
humming and breathing.

II

The sclerotic being dismantled,
a fine automaton springs downtrack.
Arises a roar,
not from any gathered,
but from the earth's five corners,
a wind,
accelerative of the hero,
no, of his image,
atomized with speed,
passing into light,
melded with the smart horizons.

The Furthest Reaches
(for Simone Weil)

The furthest reaches
are beyond sight,
beyond hearing –
perhaps they can be felt,
as background?

We imagine them
as ultimately cold,
colder than under
every winter's night,
too cold even for ice,
or as white heat,
beyond heat –
as radiation,
the shock when
the blast furnace opens.

We know them, however,
as hardness,
the reach of the bones
inside the corruptible.
They are the homeland of form.

In the moment before
being consumed,
she said, 'no,'
'here too is sense –
we must speak of this.'

Guyenne Sketch
for Ella & Tilda

I.

Stranded
from the future
pale
water tower
rising
over oak woods.

Below
deer pass
first shapes
marked on twilight
with a burnt stick.

Palaeo –
old
lithos –
stone –
and
man?

A lone pair
of halogen beams
shuttling
to the edge of town,
to Leclerc's
bath of light.

Captured
on the way
against the tree-wall

what must have been
a large hare.

II.
Birds of Prey and Passage

And so the vines were planted
and poetry began
or rather, poetry did not begin,
as here also the vines were planted,
verbiage spreading in the vineyards.

Men appeared and disappeared,
houses emptying at will,
or filled with the migratory –
space for changing voices,
protectorate of kites –
those overseers
of opportunity.

III.

The chase saves the woods,
acorns sprout under feet
of the young Navarre.
Chinese pheasant coughs
from the tapestried valley.
The deer are among
the un-Catholic vines –
never to be traded as Bordeaux,
though fifteen churches hold
just one small congregation
and no one comes to hear
Jean Calvin.

IV.

Roman

The hill-flank's burnt hide,
pieds noirs
of vines out of season,
smudged oaks,
the Curia Julia,
old Senate House,
stone and tiles,
clear in the low sun.

(Barn,
or studio,
projected time
of a youth
retired?

Connected –
wires transecting
ungenerate earth,
cables drawing
north.)

The South
laid out –
cube, sphere,
cylinder,
right domain
of a raw head
in Apulian dust,
medieval Augustus,
unreal ruler
of the octagonal
real.

Stupor
of the world.

V.

Oriflamme of sunset
in the western oaks.

On floor mulch
shade gathers,
extends from tree-feet
across the field,
swallows the land.

By night
the house besieged,
unknown cries
in the deep hours,
nosings under window,
clay printed –
the wild repassing
close to the stone,
the decommissioned
ironage.

In deeper hours
hooves and breath,
noiseless,
and *sabots,*
that leave no mark.

On Either Side

The Cards

Shuffling
the old images,
seeing if
this time
they'll come out.

In the shifts,
the subtlety
of rearrangement,
yes,
finding pleasure,
lacking
the impatience
to force it.

# of a Blank

The Digger

Was it ever
adequate?
Was it
meant to be?
Meant?

And I'm here
doing this.
This?

Working and
wondering,
never
at the same time,
never separately.

As drumbeats begin
pounding towards tomorrows:

how can what is
ever not have been?

Sudoku

And then

within the grid,
just glimpsed –
a dance

of dyads, triads,
unresolved symmetries,
patterned motion
behind the squares.

After all

is this a cage,
or a snapshot –
a little corner
in existence

at which an angel
might glance, saying,
'oh, that one?'

(never having seen it before)?

Excerpt from 'A New History of Printing' (1933)

The pursuit, by steady, methodical experimentation, of the transfer process in typesetting, had yielded notable results by the late eighties. Almost simultaneously in Paris and London (and it is probable that Berlin and Chicago were not far behind), an alternative was found to the traditional form with its heavy metal type, thanks to advances in the synthesis of new organic materials. Gossamer-light 'leaves' of type were found to 'overleaf' and bond into sheets from which clear impressions could be obtained by a process not dissimilar to that of Chinese screen-printing, thus replacing the printer's chase with a frame. The serendipity of the new process lay in its unexpected compatibility with many of the older printing presses – no great change in equipment was required, making it a matter of the utmost simplicity for a firm to 'go over' to transfer printing. But the real revolution in publication was not to occur for another decade, and this time its undisputed birthplace was London, that crucible of novelty, at the hitherto undistinguished firm of Joseph and Sons.

The story goes that in the workshops in Clerkenwell it was noticed by the master printers that a particular apprentice, given to reading the firm's productions during work hours, had transferred his surreptitious attentions from the printed pages to their 'formal' progenitor: he read the sheets of arranged type and not the print. On being alerted to this fact (and, it is surmised, having released the apprentice from his service) the director of the firm, Mr. Rupert Joseph, turned over in his mind this peculiar fact: that an earlier stage in the process of printing was capable of replacing the end of that process. Why not read the type, when it was as legible as the printed impression made from it? The calculative mind of Mr. Joseph weighed up the merits of the two media, and found itself drawn more and more to the possibilities of the form, that is, the sheet of type. It was light and durable, more durable than paper, and he was convinced that it could be produced at very little cost, should a large enough factory be established. Moreover, it possessed a physical attribute, peculiar in itself, but even more peculiar in its lending itself to certain habits of reading: it glowed softly, and seemed to encourage the reader to retreat to a twilit, private space to gaze into the patterned panel. It was less effective in direct sunlight, where a printed page held a distinct advantage, but Mr. Joseph reasoned that the outdoors and daylight, when not associated with genuine work, were the customary environment for exercise and the pursuit of health, and not, in that decade at least, a proper locus for bookish practices. And it was new, and in an age of progress, of *evolution* indeed, the 'new' automatically held a fascination for the popular mind.

There was one obvious barrier along the way of his mental explorations: sheets of type did not lend themselves to mass reproduction, the very point of the moveable type press in the first place. But here another peculiar characteristic of the new medium promised to release Mr. Joseph from this age-old condition: by laying a blank sheet of the new material over the sheet of type, any layman could, speedily and with little trouble, make a satisfactory facsimile of the page, which could then be copied again almost ad infinitum. No mechanism, no matter how ingenious, would rationalise and speed up the process (thus including a role for the manufacturer in the printing process) but the possibility of a new order of distribution, in which a customer in possession of the text and a sheet could pass on the product as they wished, intrigued Joseph, though not so much for its libertarian aspects as for its commercial radicality. Whoever had a monopoly on the new material would, by proxy, be the sole publisher in an economic system where customers did most of the production.

Mr. Rupert Joseph, soon to be *Sir Rupert Joseph,* a name whose fame has resounded throughout the world, went about securing that monopoly with the energy and ruthlessness of the Great Khan, in partnership with Sir Roderick Beecham of Lloyd's Bank. It was not long before his reach was limited only by the major national borders and even at these he did not baulk, lobbying for trade agreements to be negotiated that might extend his hold on the manufacture of the material throughout the blue-robed globe. At the same time he gathered and housed, in a specially designed building in Hertfordshire, an association of leading figures in the chemical sciences, to perfect the revolutionary material. In the hands of these Titans of the Laboratory the material proved miraculous indeed, and it was a fateful day on which Professor A.T. Saunders presented Sir Rupert with a complete edition of Gibbon's *Decline and Fall of the Roman Empire* arranged on the transfer sheets. To Sir Rupert's astonishment the full six volumes, published as one 'book', if you could call it such, occupied a depth no thicker than a single leaf of paper. As Professor Saunders so aptly put it on that historic occasion, "we will no longer read from the rough stuff of paper, but will henceforward peruse the Great Works on sheets of light". 'Sheets of light' indeed they were, which presented both another unprecedented difficulty, and an astounding possibility. In the first place they were too refined to be manipulated by coarse flesh; but by returning the frame (which had been discarded with the sheets' new role) and introducing a watch-like mechanism, connected to the sheets by cilia of gold leaf, this obstacle too was surmounted. The possibility that opened before Sir Rupert's dazzled inner eye was the inclusion of all books, indeed every text ever published, in a single volume. It was only a matter of time before it happened, and as we all know now, that time is rapidly nearing. There was one small cloud on the otherwise luminous horizon, noticed at first by the laboratory assistants, and leading to the slang coinage 'kindling' – that these successors to the book were highly flammable. Sir Rupert determined that the release of his extraordinary product would be accompanied by suitable cautionary instruction.

The effect upon the world of Joseph's Patent Luminescent Typofer, for so he dubbed his invention, was explosive. From baronet to boot catch, every stratum of society hunted the shining commodity, and a mania for swapping sheets and making collections swept the land. Bookshops and printers collapsed overnight, but on the strength of Sir Rupert's trade alone the economic vigour of Britain's Empire waxed and its tree of nations put forth new shoots. Libraries were at first appalled, but when it was realised that the space required for all the stacks and bays bearing the load of those old papery blocks could now be converted to a myriad of useful purposes, coterminous with the many societies for self-improvement and political association springing up throughout the country, the embrace of the new medium, at least among the echelons that matter, was heartfelt. The classification of the obsolescent medium soon became a binary affair: books fell into the artistic-cum-antique class, or were to be replaced by the new medium. But it was in the groves of Bohemia, among the fine artists, that the greatest shockwaves were felt, and that the final astounding property of the new medium revealed itself, like the last seal being broken on the Divine Book of the Apocalypse. It seeped as a rumour from that fairy suburb that if the layered sheets were observed from the correct angle and in the correct light, one could read *through* the text, looking down vertiginously into a mine of words as one's eye scanned along the line. This became a feverishly pursued fashion, stoked by the notion that with sufficient texts, and the inclusion of the dictionary, not only every past book, but every future book too could be seen in the depths of the panel. The gaze of the enthusiast wandered for hours down that self-reflecting tunnel of light, seeking felicitous correspondences, tracing out the formulations of the future. 'We have been freed', declared N., a sculptor of a certain notoriety, 'from the whitened phrases of the past. Had it not been for this, we would have had need of explosives. But now, we are all in possession of the unprecedented.'

The appearance of the Joseph Patent Luminescent Typofer was indeed a happy occasion, and one heralding epochal change. It truly ushered in a new chapter in, what we may now safely call, the Joseph Patent Luminescent Typofer of History, to which we are all, from Shanghai to Greenwich, witnesses. Few in the long run were the voices of dissent. A short-lived movement in philosophy and the arts, of strong aestheticist bent, bemoaned the loss of the material pleasures of the old medium: the smells, the feel of the object, the different styles of cover. It was not made clear whether the artists in question had read the books concerned. This indictment could not be levelled at the loose association referring to itself as 'dedicated readers' who, complaining in the Darwinian jargon of the day, made claim that they were being deprived of their 'habitats', and that, ironically, they found themselves isolated in a world of texts. And there are many accounts from the period – the medium, despite all its owners' precautions, still lending itself to conflagration – of the strange experience of watching a whole library, perhaps even a civilization, burn in bright seconds down to a grey nothing.

NOTES

Cover image: the 'Unfinished Obelisk' in the Quarry at Aswan, Egypt. Cropped version of photo by Diego Delso, delso.photo. License: CC BY-SA.

p.7 Iggy Pop: 'Caesar Lives'. *Classics Ireland* vol. 2 (1995)

p.9 'Savonia' refers to the southeastern Finnish district of 'Savo'. It is dominated by the million bays, islands and isthmuses of Lake Saimaa.

p.13 Epigraph from *Hamlet*. 'The Octagon' was written in 2015-2016 and includes reflections of a number of public events of that time, including the 'fiscal waterboarding' of Greece. The form was influenced by descriptions of the composer Henry Cowell's use of 'tone clusters'.

p.34 Epigraph from Heidegger's commentary on Aristotle's *De Coelo (On the Heavens)*. The Lough is a small, natural lake in Cork's southern suburbs, not far from the university campus. It is a bird sanctuary, with many species nesting on its marshy, sally-clogged central island. The writer and academic Daniel Corkery brought the nationalist revolutionary Padraig Pearse there for a walk in the early twentieth century. My father was fond of recounting the story, ending with Pearse's jibe as the punchline.

p.37 The Celtic Tiger was an economic boom period in Ireland that lasted from the mid-nineties to 2008. The nineteenth-century writer Fr. Francis Sylvester Mahony's grave lies in the grounds of St. Anne's Church, Shandon. Samuel Beckett set a scene from *Murphy* at the spot. The epigraph is from the anonymous Munster song 'Sean Ui Duibhir an Ghleanna', with the English of Trevor Joyce.

p.39 The Elysian Building is a flashy Celtic Tiger-era construction that dominates much of the eastern end of Cork City. It was more or less deserted for a long period after the economic crash of 2008. The poem descends layer by layer back through the city's history (and prehistory) and graphically mimics the shape of the glass tower at the Elysian's southern end. The poem was commissioned by Graham Allen and Billy Ramsell for a collection inspired by the building and what it represented.

p.43 J.S. Bach's *The Musical Offering* was composed in response to a challenge set by Frederick the Great of Prussia. It was published in 1747. The poem was commissioned by Maya Recordings to accompany a recording of the piece by Camerata Kilkenny.

p.49 The poem is a retelling of the ancient Greek myth of the death of Hippolytus. As with all retellings there are minor deviations from previous versions. The 'Cubism' referred to in the title refers at once to aspects of the form of the poem, the poem's titular subject-matter, and a historic period (roughly that of the institutionalisation of the Cubism of Braque and Picasso, centred on the aftermath of World War I).

p.68 The piece was written for a spoken word and performance night, 'Foaming at the Mouth', curated by Tracy Hanna and Erner Lynch at the Stag's Head in Dublin.

ACKNOWLEDGEMENTS

Versions of these poems have appeared in the following publications: *The Stinging Fly, Poetry Salzburg Review, The Irish University Review, The Elysian: Creative Responses* (Binary Press), *J.S. Bach: The Musical Offering* (Maya Recordings). 'Cork's Lough', 'Twinning' and 'J.S. Bach's Musical Offering' were previously published as part of *VIII Stepping Poems and Other Pieces* (Miami University Press, 2011). Thanks to the editors concerned.

Particular thanks to my wife Marja, children Ella, Tilda and Allu, Matti, Eeva and the Tuhkanens, the Baxters, Simpsons and the brother, Dobz and Aoife, Trevor and Owen, David Lloyd, Keith Tuma, David Toms, Fanny Howe, Randolph Healy, James Hogan, Geoff Squires, Cal Doyle, Sheila Mannix, Billy and Ailbhe, Stephen Boyd, Daragh Breen, Ger at work, Annette Dunlea, Jenny Guy, David Vichnar, and all who have provided private refuges, public fora and readership. And remembering Val Raworth.